LIVRARIAS SICILIANO

S0-APP-341

The Joy of Rio
first publishing in the United States in 1980
by Vendome Press
515, Madison Avenue, New York 10022
library of congress catalog card number 80-51190
ISBN 0-86565-055-5

© Copyright **les éditions du pacifique.** 1977, 1980
All rights reserved for all countries.
Typeset in France by Publications-Elysées.
Printed in Japan by Shumposha Photo Printing.

# The Joy of Rio

PHOTOGRAPHY
&
LAY-OUT
**BERNARD HERMANN**
TEXT
**VINICIUS DE MORAES**
**FERREIRA GULLAR**

**The Vendome Press**

New York / Paris / Lausanne

**The Joy of Rio**
First published in the United States in 1980 by The Vendome Press
515 Madison Avenue, New York, N.Y. 10022
Distributed in the United States by The Viking Press
625 Madison Avenue,
New York, N.Y. 10022
Distributed in Canada by Viking-Penguin
© Copyright Les Editions du Pacifique 1977, 1980
All rights reserved for all countries
Typeset in France by Publications-Elysées
Printed and bound in Japan by Shumposha Photo Printing


**Library of Congress Cataloging in Publication Data**

Hermann, Bernard, 1941–
  The joy of Rio.

  1. Rio de Janeiro—Description—1951—Views.
I. Moraes, Vinícius de.   II. Title.
F2646.1.H4713   1980      779'.998153      80-51190
**ISBN 0–86565–005–5**

# CONTENTS

# A self-portrait

There are many personal ways of describing a city, but we Latin Americans have the habit of seeing our cities and our people through the eyes of others. The first descriptions of our country and our people were written by European travelers and chroniclers. In the first years of our history, they arrived in Brazil, attracted by the exoticism of the recently discovered New World. Hans Spaten, the German diarist, made two voyages to Brazil in the 16th century, and during the second, fell into the hands of the Tupinamba Indians and miraculously escaped their cannibalistic rituals. His chronicles included illustrations intended to complete the description of the unknown land and the customs of its inhabitants. But the best description of Rio de Janeiro that we have is in the engravings of the French painter, Jean-Baptiste Debret, published in *Voyage pittoresque et historique au Brésil*, Paris, 1834-1839.

As time passed, and modern means of transportation were developed, distant parts of the world became more accessible. The adventurous traveler of the past has been replaced by the tourist of today who flies from one end of the world to the other. He knows in which hotel to stay and arms himself with all possible information about the city he intends to visit.

To satisfy the demands of the modern traveler, an entirely new branch of publishing has been created. The old engravings have been supplanted by color photographs.

The book we now offer to the reader's curiosity does not draw from the exoticism of the ancient chronicles, but neither does it submit to the rules of a schematic guide book. The authors do not intend to give an objective view of the city of Rio de Janeiro, merely listing historical dates and statistics. The reader will only find a few references of this kind, because it is not facts that enable one to know a city. Especially if that city is Rio de Janeiro with her beautiful scenery, contrasting life styles, and original Carioca spirit. This book has been written by two Cariocas—one by birth, the other by adoption— and is a self-portrait more than a factual portrait of the city. Rio will caress you, and sometimes, mistreat you, but she will always fascinate you and make you long to be there.

# Four centuries of youth

Rio de Janeiro sits capriciously on a thin strip of land between the mountains and the sea. It is some four centuries old, but seems as youthful as the sunburnt youngsters who bathe by its beaches and dance down its avenues during Carnival.

Though a city may reveal herself through her past, such is the brilliance of Rio's days—floating between the bay and its green hilltops—that only the present seems to exist.

The link between Rio's past and her present perhaps explains why a very special human being was born—the Carioca, for whom life, in spite of everything else, is one long holiday. It is for this purpose alone that he works and struggles. It would be an easy task to expound only on this complex city's incredible physical attractions. Some say that Rome is the most beautiful creation of man, and that Rio is the most beautiful creation of God. But man has had a say in this creation as well. In fact man and the city were created in each other's image.

## A changing city

In the 16th century, the entire production of Guanabara's sugar refineries was shipped from this simple sugar port bound for Portugal. Three centuries later Rio had become the principal commercial, political, and cultural center of Brazil, influencing the destiny of the country. This influence was innate. For even today, when the city no longer bears the title of Federal Capital nor remains the main economic center of Brazil, her influence is stronger than ever. In fact, it is Rio de Janeiro that gives the country the basic patterns of its identity. If one can speak in general terms of such a thing as a Brazilian, that person would be modeled on the Carioca—his way of speaking, his bossa-nova, his irreverence, his cunning, and his joy in life.

Rio de Janeiro's historical origins are not very different from those Latin American cities. The city resulted from a cycle of riches. Gold and diamonds first transformed Minas Gerais into the center of Brazilian economy, and Rio—the port through which these riches passed—became the seat of the colonial government. This wealth lasted for less than a century.

Next came the coffee. In the early 19th century, plantations spread throughout the Paraiba Valley and gave the city of Rio de Janeiro a new stimulus. From then onward, it never stopped growing. It was during this time that the "coffee kings" built palaces near the Quinta Imperial in Olaria, lined with marble from Carrara and designed by architects imported from

Europe; thus was created the city of Catete, nestled between marshland and jungle. Important in the development of the Carioca and the Brazilian character was the Negro slave who worked on the vast *fazendas* ("ranches") and in the sumptuous mansions. Even as a captive, the Negro managed to keep alive his culture, which can be found today in the beliefs and superstitions rooted deeply in the Brazilian spirit and in the rhythms of the folk music.

In the late 19th century, the now famous beaches of Copacabana, Ipanema, and Leblon lay deserted, separated from the town by a long line of hills. The city boundareis, after engulfing Botafogo, Cosme Velho, and the hill of Santa Tereza, reached the ancient Morro do Castelo in the north. Streetcars, first drawn by donkeys and later run on electricity, helped expand the city northward. Ponds and marshes were filled and the Mangue Canal was dug. Later, the Velho Tunnel was opened, breaking through the natural barrier of the hills and allowing the streetcar lines to reach Copacabana and Ipanema.

Rio de Janeiro entered the 20th century with more than half a million inhabitants. Since then it has mushroomed—811.400 in 1906; 1.157.800 in 1920; 2.377.400 in 1950. Must of these people were not born in Rio: they came from all over Brazil—from the Amazon jungle and the gauchos'pampas, from the drought-scorched Northeast, from the Hoias plateau, and from Minas Gerais. And through the years they married, intermarried and became Carioca, for this hospitable and carefree city turns everyone into a Carioca, no matter where he comes from.

## The Carioca legend

There are several theories on the origin of the word "Carioca". Here is the most plausible explanation: torrents of water came down the mountain, crossed the old Arcos Aqueduct and was collected in gourds by the inhabitants. As it flowed along its course it received seven names, but was called the Carioca River where it finally flowed into the sea across Flamengo Beach, from the abundance of a fish called *acari*, living in their *oca* "house" in the Tupi language): hence *acari-oca* which was shortened to *Carioca*.

As a fish needs water so a native needs to live in his city. That is, in essence, a Carioca.

An ancient legend says the Tamoio Indians, primitive inhabitants of the area, traveled down the river in their canoes, hardly cutting the surface of the water with their paddles. They believed the river could sing and also that the Indians who bathed in these waters were given greater beauty. One can imagine the large number of female visitors! And judging by the present population, there is little doubt that the legend left indelible marks. It is hard to find a more music-loving people and difficult to imagine a Carioca unable to sing or "scratch" the guitar. And it just so happens that practically all Carioca women are beautiful and elegant. Perhaps the legend is not really a legend at all. The Cariocas are extremely concerned with cleanliness, no matter what their social class or education. In fact it is very rare to find a Carioca who does not bathe two or three times a day in summer. Indeed, the Carioca River has had an important part in the building of Rio's personality.

But why Rio de Janeiro?

In 1501, a year after the discovery of Brazil by the Portuguese explorer Pedro Alvares Cabral, King Manuel of Portugal sent an expedition to trace the Brazilian coast from north to south. They were instructed to name the various geographical features after the saint's day on which they were sighted.

On January 1, 1502 the expedition anchored in a large bay which seemed to be the mouth of a large river. It happened to be the day of the Circumcision of Our Lord, but the name did not seem a fit eponym, so they decided to call the place "Rio de Janeiro" or "January River" after the month. The bay, called by the Indians "Guanapara" or "arms of the sea" became the Bay of Guanabara". It is considered by many travelers to be the most beautiful in the world.

**The charm of Rio**

The Carioca takes full pleasure in his city. He may criticize it, but he loves it dearly and feels happy only when living in the midst of its charming disorder. Although he adopts a superior attitude, the criticism of foreigners hurts him deeply. For him—in spite of the terrible summer heat, the discomfort of public transportation, the *favelas* ("slums"), and the ever-increasing delinquency—Rio is like a *femme fatale* who mistreats him, is unfaithful to him, and frequently abandons him to his fate. But without her he cannot survive.

The breath taking scenery of the sea and the mountain in close embrace, the charm of the Carioca—these help the native of Rio to forget the serious problems of the city which stem from an evident social unbalance and seem to have no immediate solution. It is painful to think that in one of the world's largest and loveliest cities, where population has reached eight million inhabitants, the problem of the *favelas* exists. In these the lower classes of the population, primarily black, live clustered together in the greatest poverty. Rio is a city that has everything, from the most beautiful to the most repugnant, from the elements that inspired *Black Orpheus*—a symbol of the musical genius of this race—to those that create fearful criminals.

The Cariocas and the Brazilians in general are not dishonest people. The Carioca is incapable of stealing for the pleasure of stealing. And if nowadays a few taxi-drivers, bartenders and waiters tend to "overcharge a bit", they take their example from abroad. They have seen the quick and unscrupulous way their foreign colleagues have made their fortunes, accustomed to the toughness and business know-how of large industrial cities. Now they too have started to use these methods with the tourists and even with the locals. But the so-called middle class is honest. Honest, but not in the English sense of the word. For example a book or newspaper seller would not dare to leave merchandise on the street in Rio as it is currently done in England, convinced that upon his return from lunch he would find it as he left it, or with cash substitued for the book or newspaper. We have not yet achieved such a degree of "civilization".

The Brazilians are a generous and good people and would never abandon or ignore anyone in need. The Carioca believes that it is always better to give a beggar something, even knowing that the plea may be a subterfuge and that the man will use the money to buy himself a drink of *cachaça* (an alcoholic drink). But he will give!

**The three fundamental M's**

You may do anything to the Carioca—take away his job, increase his daily share of sorrows, make him wait for endless hours to catch the overloaded bus home from work, dilute the milk with which he feeds his children—but he must not be deprived of the three fundamental M's in his life: Mistress, Music, and Marecanã Stadium. Without these his life is tasteless and grey.

No woman can be unhappy in Rio de Janeiro. The Carioca surrounds her with such tenderness, devotion, and love that she feels like a queen.

It is true that few other women deserve more attention than the Carioca woman. Her combination of charm, feminity, and companionship is difficult to find elsewhere. She is entirely dedicated to the opposite sex and takes constant care of her own appearance. The Carioca woman seems to leave her house prepared for love. If one woman is richer and has access to the more fashionable stores, the poorer woman is in no way discouraged. She overcomes this drawback with talent, imagination, and patience, inventing attractive garments that no fashion designer could produce with such quality, lest his prices become too exorbitant.

Her specialities are embroidered lingerie, handmade with Oriental care or with cleverly wrought lace, infinitely superior to the best any machine could produce. Her ornaments would make a well-to-do lady quite envious, in spite of yearly trips to Paris and dresses bought from Dior. For her, in this "holy war" for the opposite sex, "all is fair".

If it is possible to say that a country is as happy as the relationship between its men and women, then in spite of all its problems, Brazil is a happy country. It would be hard to find men and women who understand each other better, despite modern man's increasing confusion when confronted with his responsibilities towards women.

Music, the second "M" is a spiritual matter for the Brazilian in general and for the Carioca in particular. There is no home without music in Rio de Janeiro. In every family at least one member plays the guitar, the national instrument. Each new samba melody provides conversation for weeks. Popular composers are true idols in Rio, recognized in the streets. The Cariocas, born to sing and to dance, find the expression of their innermost feelings in song.

When the Maracanã soccer stadium was opened to the public, in 1950, and Brazil lost the World Cup to the Uruguayan team, the Brazilians were so disheartened one had the impression that the country itself had died. And people did die of sadness. Mere threats of defeat in a championship match can cause heart attacks and the despair of the public is so great that many beat their heads against the cement posts. Such is the Brazilian's passion for soccer. There is no dead end, no vacant lot, no strip of beach which the Carioca does not use for a short *pelada* or "match". And it is in Maracanã that the future stars, the future Garrinchas and Pelès, come to show off their abilities in front of an ecstatic public.

This is Rio. This is the Carioca and his city.

*Famous Pão de Açúcar ("Sugar Loaf") is
connected to Vermelha Beach by cable car.
Like the Corcovado, on which Christ the
Redeemer stands, it is one of the most beautiful
natural symbols of the city.  In the background,
the Mesa do Imperador ("Emperor's Table").
Previous double page: Rio de Janeiro seen
from the Alto de Corcovado, in the background,
the lights of Guanabara Bay.*

*Copacabana Beach became popularly known as "The Pearl Necklace". It was the "in" beach of the thirties and forties. Copacabana, with a population of half a million inhabitants crowded into tall apartment buildings, is the most densely populated district in the world. Previous double page: in the background, Copacabana Beach; to the left, Urca Beach; to the right, Botafogo Bay.*

The variety of Rio's scenery
is amazing: sea and mountain,
forests and parks, modern
skyscrapers and old colonial
houses. From Tijuca Forest
one can see the top of Christ
the Redeemer on the
Corcovado. The waterfall,
"Bridal Veil," is a traditional
meeting place for lovers.
Lovely cottages were built
along the forest lanes where
carriages still pass. Previous
double page: the commercial
and administrative center of
Rio seen from the other side
of the bay in the early hours
of the morning.

*For the visitor arriving by boat, the
sight of Rio is breathtaking. Past the
islands of Guanabara Bay, the
Atlantic beaches and the mountains
offer a superb spectacle.*

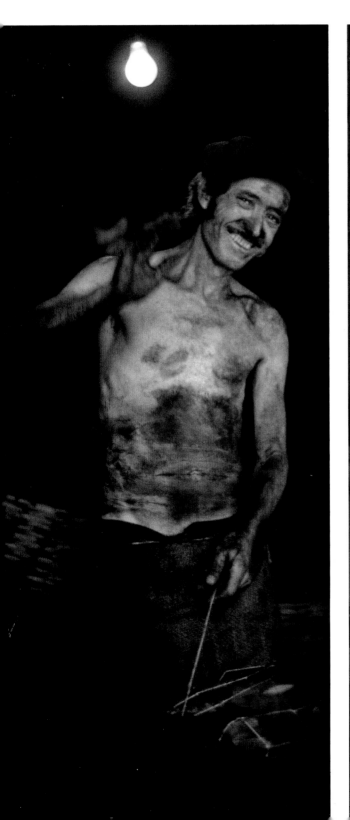

*The Carioca are a happy and carefree people, in spite of all their problems, mostly stemming from the population explosion and the poor public transportation. They possess a strong sense of self-criticism and an incredible wit which transforms everything into a joke. The Carioca race has produced that unique creature: the beautiful Carioca woman.*

*Another enchanting aspect of the city is the informality of its inhabitants. Their warm welcome to visitors from all over the world makes everyone feel at home. Whites, blacks, mulattos —all get along beautifully. Well known poets musicians and painters of Brazil have long celebrated the unique beauty of the mulatta. Her physical charm and her natural aptitude for dancing and singing make her absolutely irresistible.*

# The girls from Ipanema

The Carioca beaches are famous throughout the world for their beauty. But the first early settlers sought the higher places to found their cities for reasons of protection and health. In addition the humid and hot climate of the lowlands, especially in summer, was far less attractive than the mountains, constantly aired by cool sea breezes.

But what seemed right to the government did not always seem right to the people. Climbing the steep sides of the hills was difficult and people settled in the lowlands. There they could easily buy the supplies they required. Canoes from farms and sugar factories brought goods and equipment to the beach, and small shops started opening. In this way the Piaçava Beach became inhabited. Huts of sticks and stones were put up, and the first city road was built. Although the houses were set up without any order, they always faced the sea.

## The first bathers

By the middle of the 19th century, sea bathing became a polular entertainment; the royal family had long since given its approval. Dom Joao VI, the Portuguese Prince Regent, used to bathe in the sea at Cajú Beach, now a favorite in the northern zone of the city. But he did not venture very far out, and a special sort of box was built which could float on the waves without drifting from the shore. Gastao Cruls in *Aparência do Rio de Janeiro* says, "In Botafogo, no such precautions were taken because the waves were not that strong. Dona Carlota and her daughters preferred it here. Dom Pedro instead chose Flamengo Beach and used to undress in the house of the English Consul".

It is curious and almost ridiculous for us to see the photographs of the first bathing costumes of the twenties, their horizontal colored stripes covering the so-called flappers down to their ankles. Our grand-parent's would be scandalized if they could see the bathing suits of today—not only is the bikini already out of fashion, but those tiny pieces of cloth hardly cover young bathers at Ipanema or Leblon and are just enough to keep them from being entirely naked. And in the Carioca spirit, that makes fun of all things, this invention has been named the "band-aid".

The beaches have an important role in the history of Rio. One may speak of the "Copacabana generation", which in the thirties and forties was celebrated in prose and verse. They ate, played ball on the sand and engaged in homeric feats mostly forced on them by others wanting to see some action.

They gave birth to the Cafageste groupe, famous among the Bohemians of the district.

It was formed by executives and millionaires athletic, euphoric, available to women, and ready for adventure. Their territory consisted of three miles of beach, covered with sparkling white sand and beaten by a harsh and frequently dangerous sea. Fine swimmers would launch themselves from the crest of a wave, to "kill an alligator" they used to call it, and land quite roughly on the beach.

The thirties were above all a time of building speculation. Soon skyscrapers sprouted among the low houses and palatial homes along the coastline, creating a kind of cement wall almost entirely cutting off the green, pleasant view of the mountains. With the new arrivals pouring in, bars and restaurants increased in number. Some became famous like *Michel, 39,* or *Alcazar,* where the poets and writers of the time met at night, or *Tudo Azul* and later *Girau.* The most famous of all were *Le Bon Gourmet,* where the first *bossa nova* show was presented, and *Zum-Zum,* which in 1965 became the exclusive meeting place for the people of the southern zone, and especially of Copacabana, Ipanema, and Leblon. The great majority of new composers, singers, and musicians passed through them, the "kings" of *bossa-nova*—Antonio Carlos Jobim, Joao Gilberto, Baden Powell, and Carlos Lira.

## Copacabana and Ipanema

In the fifties Copacabana, becoming more and more crowded, gave way in popularity to Ipanema, then a quiet neighborly district. There, among the writers and musicians that frequently met at the Veloso Bar or in Tom Jobim's apartment on Nascimento Silva Street, the *bossa nova* was born. It has not only made Brazilian music famous, but also the district and beach of Ipanema with the song "Garota de Ipanema" ("The Girl from Ipanema") by Tom and Vinicius. It was written for the play, *Orfeu Negro* (Black Orpheus) which was staged in 1956 at the Teatro Municipal with scenery by the architect Oscar Niemeyer. Ipanema became fashionable; and its bars: *Jangadeiro, Zeppelin, Pizzaiolo,* where the artists and "beautiful people" got together before or after bathing, became famous. Some parts of the Ipanema Beach may be described by the kind of people who frequent them: at Castelinho young girls in the latest beach fashions and sunglasses, fashions that make them lovelier and cover them less; at Montenegro, the young intellectuals, directors, actors, and actresses of the *Cinema Novo.* Even though the population in this district grew rapidly, the family feeling remained. Every New Year's Eve everyone got together for a special celebration called the Jaguar Ball. From this same Group sprang *O Pasquim,* a comic newspaper which through its wit and irreverence, renewed the language of the Brazilian press and helped promote the folklore of Ipanema characters, customs, and slang.

By the early seventies many changes had taken place in Ipanema. Where the Jangadeiro once stood, an apartment building was erected; the Zeppelin became a bar for snobs; and even the Veloso went with the tide and changed its name to Garota de Ipanema. A new generation has appeared—teenagers whose craze is surfing and the modern pop groups. But the older generation has not relinquished its hold. Faithful to its traditions and to the samba, the Ipanema Band was created and has now become an indispensable part of the Carnival in the Southern zone of the city.

Leblon Beach is an extension of Ipanema and for many years was a kind of suburb of that famous district. Many of its inhabitants would walk over a mile down to Ipanema rather than bathe by their own beach. Lately Leblon has become part of the bohemian history of the southern zone.

But times have changed and the growth of the southern zone has forced another way of life upon its inhabitants. Along the coastline to the south new hotels, houses and residential areas are rapidly being built reflecting the modern, urbanistic concept of the great Lucio Costa. It makes one think of his Brasilia rather of the Rio one is accustomed to seeing.

As the city spread southward, car traffic increased and new lanes had to be added to the Avenida Atlantica. This was accomplished without encroaching on the beaches which remain as wide as ever. Adjacent to the well-known mosaic sidewalks that are Copacabana's pride the beach attracts the most beautiful women in the world all year round, and especially during the long summer season.

The beaches of Rio de Janeiro, and in particular those of the southern zone, show some of the more curious aspects of Carioca life and its basically friendly nature. In a way they represent the younger, more modern spirit of the city. Lifeguards, beach cleaners, kite and ice-cream sellers are popular figures on these golden beaches.

The Carioca cannot live
without soccer or the samba,
nor can he live without the
beach. The number of people
on the beaches during the
summer is incredible and form
a profitable clientele for local
crafts such as straw hats, to
avoid sunstroke on very hot
days. Kite sellers have sure
customers in the children who
cannot resist seeing kites
floating against the sun.

The slum dwellers in the southern zone have always found a way to earn a living: the women are employed as maids and serve in the wealthier households; the men go to sell hats, drinks and ice-cream on the beaches. Lemonade, iced maté and slices of watermelon, besides being thirst-quenching, have become part of the pleasures of the Carioca beaches.

*During the day, fishermen are not a frequen. sight, but at dawn one can see them returning to the beaches, dragging their fish-laden nets. Many housewives come to the beach to buy fresh fish for lunch. Previous double page: c summer sunset at Copacabana Beach*

*When Copacabana Beach was difficult to reach and practically deserted, the first fisher villages sprang up. The fishermen lived in simple huts and sold their catch at the markets of Praça Quinze. Today, with the appearance of a modern fishing industry, the old-fashioned fishermen are slowly disappearing.*

*A typical creature of the tropics, the Carioca woman goes to the beach to show off the beauty of her body. There she displays the elegance and good taste that are an essential part of her charm. Previous double page: the crowded Ipanema Beach on a sunny Sunday.*

*The new generation of the southern zone enjoys the luxury of surfing. The many-colored surf boards add a bright note to the beach and the championships that take place several times a year are yet another attraction for Cariocas and visitors alike.*

In this bar, formerly called "*Veloso*" and today known as "*Garota de Ipanema*," the first musicians and poets who were to make the district famous got together and wrote many of their famous songs. The song, "*The Girl from Ipanema*" was born here and dedicated to the garotas ("*girls*") who spend their summers at Ipanema Beach. Some things have changed— the Ipanema girl of today is far more conscious of her charms and far more sophisticated.

*"How nice to show off at the beach."* The words of this song tell of the Carioca philosophy that gave birth to the tanga or string bikini, popularly called a *"band-aid"*.

*Rio by night is fascinating, like an exotic gem shining in the tropical darkness, dark as the skin of many Brazilians, like this* maté *vendor who later in the year will be seen dancing and playing the tambourine in a samba club during the crazy days of Carnival.*

# A difficult city

In 1549, Tomé de Souza, first Governor General of Brazil said of Rio, "Charming is the only fitting description". This was doubtlessly what the French soldiers under the command of Nicolas Durand de Villegaignon thought when they settled in Rio in 1555 with the intention of founding a colony. This colony, the "French Antarctica", became a base for the exploitation of the *pau-brazil*, a reddish wood used in dyes, which gave its name to the country, and spices which were in great demand in Europe at the time.

Evidently King Dom Sebastiao of Portugal did not approve of these plans. In 1557 he sent his third Governor General, Mem de Sá, to Brazil with the order to rid Rio de Janeiro of the French. By then Villegaignon has already fortified the island at the entrance to Guanabara Bay, where the fortress of Lage stands today. Later he built Coligny Fort on the Island of Serigipe, now called Villegaignon in his honor. Mem de Sá destroyed the fort in 1560 and forced the French to take refuge inland. But it was only in 1565 with the arrival of his nephew, Estacio de Sá, that the French were defeated. Estacio reached Guanabara in February, to find the French had reassembled their forces after their first encounter with his uncle. On March 1st, he dropped anchor at the foot of Mount Cara de Cao and with his 300 men founded the city.

On that same day he entreated his soldiers to overcome the surrounding enemy troops, claiming that these were "not as hard to conquer as the hills or as difficult to cross as the ocean". But the French were not intimidated and returned in 1695, under the orders of De Gennes. Again they were repelled. They tried once more in 1710 with François Duclerc et Duguay-Trouin who proved much harder to repulse. The Portuguese Governor of the time, Castro Moraes, went down in history for having defended his city with such determination.

## Rio today

More than four centuries have passed since the foundation of the city. Let us see what the city looks like today.

Rio spreads out over the hills and mountains, immersed in a splendor of green. The city overtook the lowlands and filled in the marshes that separated it from the interior. But it was the coastal area that became the center fo the city. From the Gloria to the Leblon district through Niemeyer Avenue and onwards to the Bandeirantes district rises an endless line of houses and skyscrapers. Looking down, one sees the Bay of Guanabara up to the Botafogo district, and further on the Atlantic Ocean with its far off islands floating in the inviting, green-blue waters.

Although tempting, those waters are dangerous for the inexperienced swimmer.

Rio was built on land, cut by mountains, hills, forests, streams, valleys, and a large salt water lake, the Lagoa Rodrigo de Freitas. It is divided in two areas, North and South, separated by the banking district, the site of most government offices. Many Cariocas have never left the area in which they were born. The only means of passage to the center and northern area of the city from the more densely populated districts of the south (Copacabana, Ipanema, Leblon, Gavea, and Lagoa) are several tunnels dug through the mountain. In Copacabana, a city within a city, there are many who spend years before "going through the tunnel". On top of the mountain that divides the city, sit the *favelas,* quietly settled in their misery. They bear the names of the granite hills to which they cling; strange, suggestive names like Catacumba ("catacombs"), Sossego ("tranquility"), Esqueleto ("skeleton"), Cantagalo ("cock's crow"), Pasmado ("astonished"), Quinta do Céu ("heaven's farm").

**Problems and pleasure**

Universally famous Copacabana—with its beach, luxury hotels, bars, night-clubs, and intense night life—is in fact a real urban cancer. Brazilian architects and city planners are working toward the urban renewal of Rio for the year 2000. With a present population of half a million inhabitants, the most densely populated area per square kilometer in the world, life becomes unbearable for families huddled in their small apartments. Beautiful Copacabana has an ever increasing percentage of juvenile delinquency and prostitution as the younger family members take to the streets. And the streets, in Copacabana as in city streets everywhere, are poor places of learning for our youth.

Yet, at the same time, a new generation is forming in Copacabana, Ipanema, and Leblon—wiser and more beautiful than that of half a century ago. The happy combination of sun and sea and modern foods richer in proteins and vitamins has produced splendid men and women in the last two generations. On the beaches during the sunbathing hours, they are a feast for the eyes.

Rio cannot offer as comfortable accommodations and public transportation as London, Paris or New York, but its natural attractions compensate for this lack.

Let the visitor look out over Rio from the top of the Corcovado where the superb, granite pedestal and colossal statue of Christ the Redeemer, stands with open arms blessing the city. This beautiful green hilltop, at the crest of the Carioca range over 2,000 feet above sea level, offers an incomparable spectacle on one side the Chinese View, with its old Oriental kiosk; on the other, the Mesa do Imperador ("emperor's table"), named for its shape, with land and ocean spreading out as far as the horizon.

The Pâo de Açucar (Sugar Loaf) is internationally famous as the symbol of Rio de Janeiro. Its cable car crosses an abyss almost a mile deep. Like the Tower of London, the Empire State Building in New York or the Eiffel Tower in Paris, the Pâo de Açucar is a tourist's must.

This beautiful mountain is the pride of the Carioca, rising as it does from the Bay of Guanabara. It is also a popular tryst on whose heights lovers exchange kisses and secrets.

But no spectacle can surpass that from the top of Mirante Dona Marta, right in the heart of the city. All the buildings, the mountains, the sea, the islands, and the infinite blue and liquid horizon lie at the spectator's feet. As he gazes on this splendor the tourist forgets bad hotel service and exorbitant prices.

The Bay of Guanabara has over one hundred islands making the arrival in Rio by boat a fantastic treat. Of all these islands, three are of special importance to the Carioca: Brocoió, with its beautiful gardens; Ilha do Governador ("Governor's Island"), connected to the city by a bridge and on which Galeao International Airport was built; and Paquetá, also known as "Lover's Island" or "Pearl of Guanabara", a favorite place of the Carioca for a romantic weekend or a Sunday picnic. One of the nicest spots to visit in Rio is the Botanical Garden at Gavea. It was created by Dom Joaó VI in 1808, with a fabulous walk lined with Imperial palm trees and beautiful and mysterious mayflowers that open (only once a year) during the month that gives them their name.

Rio is the birthplace of the most famous Brazilian architects: Lúcio Costa, Oscar Niemeyer, Carlos Leao, Sergio Bernardes, Mauricio Roberto. There are very few of their creations, in the city itself, except the Palácio da Cultura, the residential area of Guinle Park, and the Museum of Modern Art. Other masterpieces must be sought in the maze of ordinary buildings that have begun spoiling the Carioca scenery.

Recently a gigantic bridge was built over the Bay of Guanabara, connecting Rio with the city of Niteroi. This was an important step toward the unification of the former Brazilian capital with the State of Rio de Janeiro. A recent law has strengthened this unity by transforming Rio into the capital of a new and important federal zone.

Built in the Roman style, with a double row of 42 arches, the ancient Arcos Aqueduct (1744-1750) was later transformed into a viaduct. Today, the only streetcar line that goes from the center of town to the Santa Tereza district runs across it. An exclusive residential area, Santa Tereza is the favorite district of wealthy foreigners, not only because of its milder climate but also because of its traditional architecture.
*Previous double page:*
*In the background,*
*Christ the Redeemer.*

Tradition and subtle poetry
are still part of this great city.
The visitor is often surprised
to find this hidden aspect of
Rio. In places like Santa
Tereza or Cosme Velho, time
flows slowly and silently. On
the right: the Largo do
Boticario, with the colorful
façades of its colonial
buildings, constitutes one of
the most beautiful architectura[l]
sites of old Rio. It is now
protected by the National
Artistic and Historic
Preservation Department.

In Rio there is a mixture of the modern and the
traditional. The buildings of yesterday and
today are found side by side thus giving the
city its own unique style. Below: Fiscal Island
in Guanabara Bay where the last Imperial
Ball, with all its grandeur, was held

*Confeitaria Colombo with its mirrors and chandeliers and "Art Nouveau" setting was for many years the favorite tea shop of the rich families, the intellectuals, and the young dandies of Carioca society. They would get together to talk, drink, and eat the delicious pastries that were an important factor in Colombo's success. For another kind of treat, the visitor can try the* bolos *and* churrasquinhos *that the Bahianas sell on any street corner in the city.*

*Maracanã, the largest soccer stadium in the world, seats ove 200,000 people. It was built in record time for the World Championship of 1950. Previous double page: the Aterro da Gloria, with the Parcinha Monument and the Museum of Modern Art. In th background is the new bridge over the bay.*

Open air markets are springing up since the existing grocery stores do not adequately supply the growing population. In certain streets and on certain days of the week, the markets are set up at dawn and taken down by noon. There the people can purchase fresh fruit and vegetables brought from the fertile outskirts surrounding Rio. Previous double page: a slum clings to a low hill in the northern zone.

Rio's Zoological Gardens were once the private property of Baron de Drummond. To help with the upkeep of the zoo, at the turn of the century the Baron invented a game called jogo-do-bicho, *a kind of lottery which became popular throughout the country. Although now forbidden, the craze for this game continues among its many devotees.*

There comes a time when
every great city comes to a halt
and gives its citizens a chance
to take it easy. They relax,
play cards, or just sit and think
about life in general. And when
they do, the street artists—
fire-eaters and musicians
playing exotic instruments go
to work to entertain them.
Previous double page:
The Morro da Urca
and the Sugar Loaf.

*The Central Fire Station is opposite the Campo de Santana, a beautiful, tree-filled park, ideal for those who seek peace and quiet.*

*The Alto do Corcovado, where Christ the Redeemer stands, is a must for tourists. Corcovado can be reached by cable car and offers a splendid view of Rio and Guanabara Bay from over two thousand feet up.*

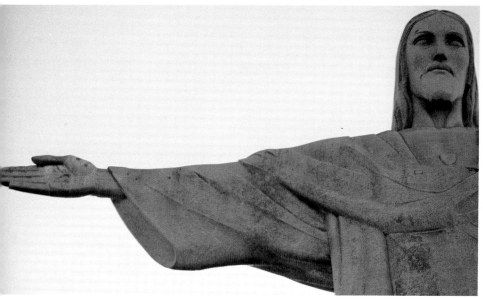

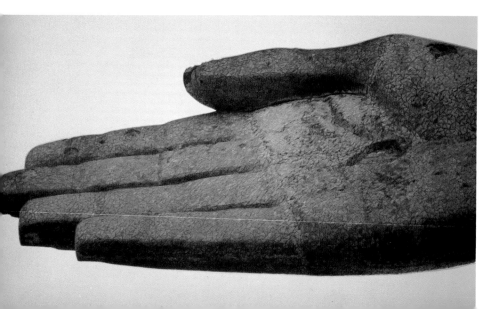

The statue of Christ the Redeemer with its 115 feet height is one of the major symbols of the city. The work of the French sculptor, Paul Landowsky, this monument was inaugurated in 1931. Its system of illumination was switched on in Rome by Marconi, the inventor of the telegraph,
by radio waves.

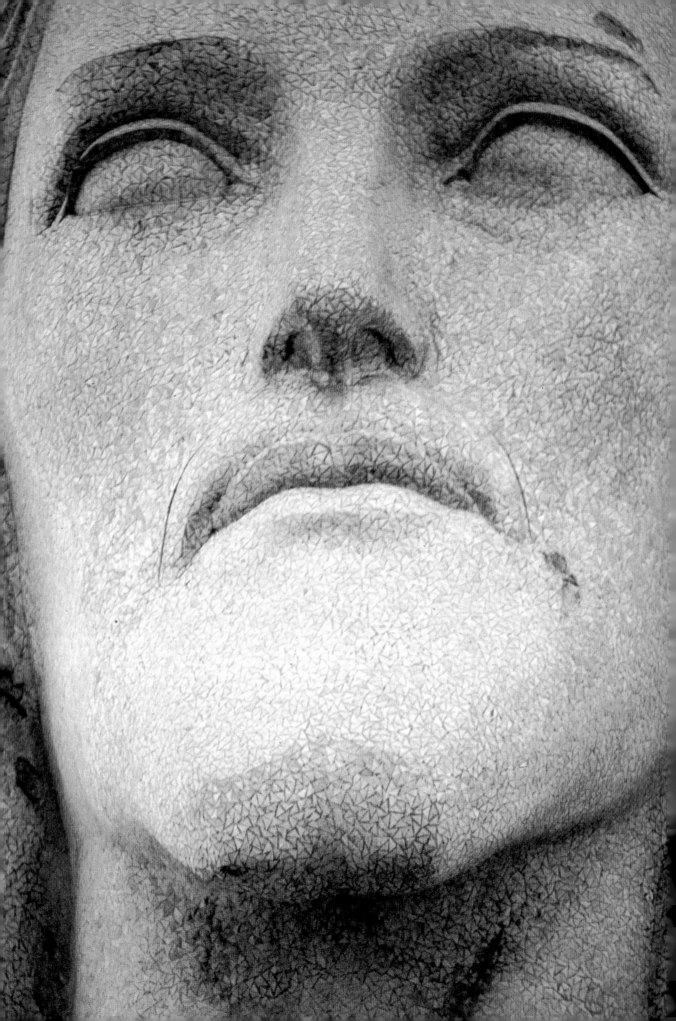

*A strip of land between the ocean and Lake Rodrigo de Freitas, Ipanema appears to float amoung azure seas. Famous throughout the world, Ipanema is merely seven blocks wide and twelve blocks long. Due to its location and size, this is one of the most expensive places in the world to buy land.*

The Botanical Garden, previously known a
Horto Real ("Royal Garden"), was create
in 1808 by Prince Regent Dom João VI. It i
famous for its paths of imperial palmtrees
All the palmtrees of this kind in Rio ar
offsprings of the first one which wa
planted by the Emperor himsel

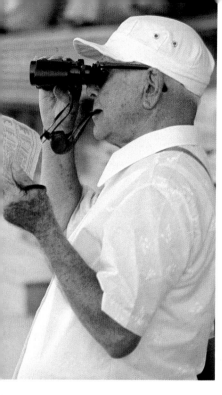

The Jockey Club, founded in
1868, was located in the
northern zone near Estação de
São Francisco Xavier until
1871. Then it moved to the
Gávea district. The present
race track was inaugurated in
1926 and was a copy of the
famous Longchamps race track
in Paris as part of the district's
improvements made at the time.
The annual Grand Prix Brazil
brings the cream of high society
to the Jockey Club. Following
double page: at the very doors
of the consumer society, half
hidden by billboards, the slums
are an undisguised reminder of
class differences.

# Gods and demons

Brazil is a Catholic country, but Brazilian Catholics go to confession on Sunday only to sin again the following day. And the Brazilian's greatest sin is the most comprehensive and agreable of them all—the sin of the flesh.

This casual and permissive Catholicism is at the core of the ethnic mixture that makes Brazil one of the most complete racial democracies in the world. The Portuguese settler was charmed by the Indian and the Negro women. The Carioca attributes to him that uniquely beautiful and graceful creation: the Brazilian mulatta.

Yet, the Brazilian people could not be materialistic *without* a religion. There exist today remnants of deep religious roots of three races—white, Indian and Negro. For the Brazilian, religion is a spiritual crutch, a proof of his own existence. It allows him to exercise with remorse, in a better and more agreable way, his human and often sub-human condition. The terrific growth in Brazilian population is one of the highest in the world. Perhaps it is because the hunger for sex is more easily satiated than the hunger for food.

## The Candomble

The *Candomblé* of Bahia may become the most popular and widespread religion in Brazil. When African captives were forced to accompany their masters to Catholic services, the slaves slowly adapted the Christian ethic yet succeeded in preserving their own gods—an astounding proof of originality, character, and will power. The African divinities, *Orixás,* were given the names of some of the principal saints of the Catholic Church. This enabled the Negroes to worship them without bringing on their master's wrath. It is interesting to note that American Negroes, though coming from the same African regions as the Brazilian slaves, allowed their gods practically to disappear. The Protestant faith does not permit image worship, and North American Negroes were forced to abandon their religion to take up that of their masters.

Bahia was the first coastal region to which slaves were brought. In that one area were concentrated the highest number of Jêje-Natô Orixas, mythological source of the Bahia Candomblé sect, considered the purest and nearest to its African roots. Negroes of Bantu origin from Angola, who came to Rio de Janeiro originated the Umbanda sect. This sect was associated with the Candomblé beliefs but was mingled with Catholicism, Oriental ideology, Allan Kardec's spiritism, and local Indian religions.

Candomblé spread out toward Pernambuco, Maranhao, and Rio Grande do Sul; Macumba and Umbanda occupied the area of Rio, the State of Rio, which are now one state, Sao Paulo, and to a certain point Minas Gerais.

In Rio de Janeiro the most important is the Umbanda sect. It was formerly called Macumba, a word used to designate all sects if African origin. Today, some thirty million followers of the Umbanda rites meet in more than one hundred thousand *terreiros* ("temples"). Twenty-two thousand of these temples are in Rio alone.

Another offshoot of the ancient Macumba is the Quimbanda sect, usually despised by the Candomblé and Umbanda because it allows the practice of evil through *despachos* ("spells"). Sometimes these spells cause death. There are Quimbanda sorcerers who cast such spells. One of the more common spells for causing death consists of leaving a small, wax doll stuck with pins in the house of the person on whom the spell has been cast—a practice that is also common in Haitian voodoo.

## The Umbanda

Even if the Umbanda evolved from the Candomblé, the names of saints given to African gods sometimes differ. It depends in which area the sect settled. For example, the God Xango corresponds to Saint Jerome in the Candomblé and to Saint Michael in the Umbanda.

The Umbanda divinities are divided into seven groups and work with the aid of spirits. The seven groups are, as follows:

— *Oxala* is the God of creation, who corresponds in Catholicism to Jesus-Christ. The only one above him is his Father, Olorum, God supreme and lord of the heavens who never shows himself and possesses no cult of his own. *Oxala* is an androgynous deity, dressed all in white. His *omala* ("divine nourishment") must also be white, like corn or unsalted cornmeal, white doves, or goat. In Oxala's *peji* ("sanctuary") his fetishes are lead rings and cowrie shells once used as money in ancient Africa. These are also used as instruments at seances conducted exclusively by ministers of the temples. *Oxala* corresponds to the most popular cult in Bahia, Our Lord of Bonfim, whose beautiful church is in the city of Salvador, capital of the state. His symbol is the shepherd's staff he leans upon during ritual dances. His day is Friday.

— *Iemanjá*, mother of the waters and of all the Orixás ("saints") and the wife of Oxalá, is the most mysterious of all goddesses. Many legends tell of how she lures fishermen and sailors into her wonderful underwater world with her singing. Her symbols are the fan and the sword. Her food is goat, chicken, and Angolan fowl; as well as duck and *acaçá* (a rice flour soup). She is coquettish, and the offerings that are thrown into the sea in her honor are mainly cosmetics, perfumes, and flowers, preferably in her own colors of white, blue or pink.

This must be done on January 1st, her day according to Umbanda. The Candomblé of Bahia celebrate it on February 2nd. She can be likened to Our Lady, under the several names of Mother of Christ.

— *Ogum* is the god of iron, war, and fighting. He shares Thursday with his brother *Oxossi.* His color is dark blue. He dresses in scarlet and wears green and white bracelets. He eats special food called *era* made of ox head and spoiled meat. His symbol is any piece of iron, even a sword. His fellow, in Bahia is Saint Antony, and in Rio Saint George.

— *Oxossi* is the god of hunting and forests whose mysteries he guards. His symbols are the bow and arrow and all other weapons used by hunters. His color is light blue; his animals are the cock and the ram; his food is *acho-cho* made of corn, In Bahia, he is Saint George and In Rio, Saint Sebastian, patron saint of the city.

— *Xango* is the warrior god of tempests, lightening and rain. With his father *Oxala,* he is the most popular and admired god. His foods are cock, billy goat, ram, ox tail, turtle and water cress. The beads of his necklace are red and white, and he wears a tin bracelet. His fetish is called *bipene.* In Bahia he is Saint Jerome and Saint Barbara, and in the south, Saint Michael. His day is Wednesday. His ritual dance is considered the most beautiful of all the cults.

— The Oriental line is an occult sect led by Saint John the Baptist.

— The African line is formed by the spirits of Negro ancients who enter the Quimbanda temples to interfere with the activities there. The patron saint is Saint Cyprian.

In Rio, the feast of Iemanjà falls on December 31. The Umbandista *ritual starts on th beaches at midnight and continues until daybreak. The faithful arrive dressed in white and bring drums, ritual instruments and gifts for the Queen of the Sea and are joined by the inhabitants of the neighboring zones.*

*Dancing and singing, worshippers pay hommage to Iemanjà, "mother of the waters," who waits at the bottom of the sea for the offerings. Flowers, combs, mirrors, necklaces and bottles of perfume are thrown into the sea. If a gift drifts back to shore, this means that Iemanjà has not accepted it.*

*Originating in the African rituals brought over by the slaves, the* Umbanda *religion is a combination of the teachings of Allan Kardec, occultism, Catholicism and native Indian ceremonies. Some thirty million people practice* Umbanda, Candomble *or one of their offshoots.*

Many shops in Rio sell articles
for the Umbandista rituals.
Apart from the religious
statues which show a marked
African influence, these shops
also sell herbs, magic potions,
incense, colorful necklaces,
candles, and bowls in which
offerings are made to the gods.
Previous double page: the
Children of Jehova are being
baptized in the waters
of the Imprensa Grotto.

*Dating from the XVII century, the Benedictine convent of Sao Benito is perhaps the finest and best-preserved religious monument in Rio de Janeiro. The high altar, with its rich gilt carving, is typical of Brazilian baroque.*

*Not all is samba and sensuality in the Carnival capital. Even though the Carioca is more superstitious than mystical, he has a profound religious feeling. During Carnival, many seek the haven of cloisters. Following double page: on January 20th a procession of the faithful is carrying a statue of Saint Sebastian on their shoulders.*

# Carnival

Just as Brazil was "born" on April 21, 1500 ("two weeks after Carnival", to quote the Carnival march by Lamartine Babo) so does Carnival have its birth date on February 1854. Before Carnival, Brazilians had a celebration called *entrudo* consisting of real street battles. Although the weapons were only flour and water, the battles often degenerated into physical combat which sometimes resulted in death. In Rio Grande do Norte, Father Lustosa, was literally drenched in the middle of the street. In view of such incidents, the chief of police of Rio passed an ordinance in 1853 forbidding *entrudo* and threatening jail to whoever persisted. The following year whole families set up barriers in the streets. Thus protected they went out to celebrate Carnival, dancing and singing in the open.

The first important Carioca Carnival took place in 1855. In January of that year the press appealed to the people, principally to the wealthier families, to participate in the festivities. Doctors, lawyers, journalists, military men, high public officials, and land owners set the tone, and with their support ensured the success of Carnival.

The entire city worked toward one goal. Shops that sold or rented costumes flourished. Women spent days and nights sewing for clowns, harlequins and the like. On Carnival Sunday, the Emperor and the royal family watched the Carnival parade from the balcony of the palace. Although Carnival has undergone many changes, its feeling of brotherhood has remained constant. For this brief period every year all class differences disappear.

### The origins of Carnival

In 1870 the first parade by the "Big Companies" was organized. This was to become the center of attraction of all future Carnivals until the arrival of the *escolas de samba* (samba schools or clubs) that today dominate the show. But before the samba school, the samba itself had to be born. Its beginnings can be traced back to the twenties at Tia Ciata's, in Praça Once, where some of the most important Brazilian musicians, like Pixinguinha and Donga, used to get together. In the Estacio district, the famous black composer, Ismael Silva, founded the first *escola-de-samba* that initially bore the name of *Deixa Falar* ("let them talk"). The groups became more numerous, until they are today the greatest popular show in the world. The three *escola-de-samba* parades on Carnival Sunday in Rio include more than forty thousand people, dancing, singing, and playing musical instruments and dressed in extraordinary, fantastic costumes. Each parade lasts throughout the night and into the morning.

The competition for musical supremacy during Carnival has given rise, among popular composers, to wonderful specialists in Carnival music. They spend all year creating the principal *piadas* (consisting of spicy anecdotes, comic sketches, witty remarks, fads, words in vogue, political happenings, and all sorts of city gossip). These *piadas* reflect the life of the city and matters of public interest. Set to music during the festivities, they serve as a spark to set the whole city dancing and singing for three uninterrupted days. According to sociologists and psychologists, this pure joy and total liberty is a formidable escape valve for the traumas and neuroses brought on by daily stress. All is forgotten. Housemaids, factory workers, clerks, hoodlums from the slums and criminals forsake their cares for 72 hours and "go crazy". In groups that vary in size from the *blocos de sujos* (bands of street urchins) of only a few people to the *escolas-de-samba* of thousands of dancers they leave their favelas on the mountain, or their housing projects or their wretched rooms in their masters' homes and give themselves over, body and soul, to dancing and singing. For those few days they overcome their social misfortunes, their class problems, and the humiliations of their plebeian existence. Often they spend all the money they have saved over the year. Everyone, the great majority black or mulatto, dress themselves in such rich costumes that they look like kings, queens or noblemen from around the world. Madame Pompadour, the Marquise of Santos, and other court favorites of French and Portuguese kings parade down the Presidente Vargas and Rio Branco avenues, the luxurious costumes clothing beautiful bodies full of grace and majesty.

### A dream come true

During Carnival, the Carioca mulatta reigns as absolute queen. Her beauty, celebrated in prose and verse by so many writers, poets, and musicians and immortalized on canvas by the best Brazilian painters is a symbol of Brazil's racial democracy. It is naive to suppose that there is no racial prejudice in Brazil. Prejudice exists in the upper classes and among certain groups of parvenus. The rapid industrial growth in the city of Sao Paulo, where European immigrants became rich quickly, brought a new form of snobbism based on money. But except for certain balls—at the Teatro Municipal or the Copacabana Hotel, whose high-priced tickets only the rich can afford—during Carnival the people black and white, go about arm-in-arm in the spirit of brotherhood. Unlike the small contribution of the native Indians to Brazilian culture, the contribution by blacks is of fundamental importance, especially in music. The *samba carioca,* known throughout the world through the *bossa-nova* was created when the black *batucada* ("African dance") merged with tunes composed by black and white city musicians. The *bossa-nova* represents the latest form in the evolution of the *samba carioca;* a modern form, a richer more harmonious form of the tradional samba and instrumentally more complete. Created by professionals who possess a thorough understanding of musical expression, the *bossa-nova* represents an updating of the samba but leaves intact the authenticity of its rhythm and poetry.

**The sadness of bliss**

The samba "Happiness", describes the inner sadness resulting from the brief, social liberation of the lower classes during the festivities of Carnival :

Sadness has no end...
Happiness has.
The happiness of the poor is like
Carnival's great illusion.
People work all year round,
For a moment of dreams,
To build up the fantasy
Of being king, pirate, or gardener,
And all is over on Wednesday.

When parades first crossed the city from one end to the other, large numbers of people stopped their dancing and instead became spectators watching the procession of carriages and costumes. The street Carnival cooled down a little. This trend seemed to grow with the years, and the Carnival in the districts became less important, as the organized parades became more popular. But the Carnival spirit of the Carioca is invincible. Some ten years ago the Banda da Ipanema was formed, and creation of similar bands in Copacabana, Leme, Largo do Machado, and Tijuca has given new blood to the Carnival spirit in the districts.

The truth is that in all large cities popular festivities tend to disappear. In this Rio is an exception, because it would be impossible to imagine Rio without the Carnival.

*Carnival, a holiday for all, is also a livelihoo*
*for many. Because of the celebration, littl*
*shops are opened that sell masks, bea*
*necklaces, paper garlands, confetti and flag*
*Hundreds of workshops are kept busy sewin*
*fantastic creations for the samba clubs, som*
*producing fine works of ar*

*Carnival in the streets—from the organized parades and the* escolas-de-samba *to the thousands of individuals who join in spontaneously—is a truly popular celebration. The motto of the young is: the more laughter and the less clothing the better!*

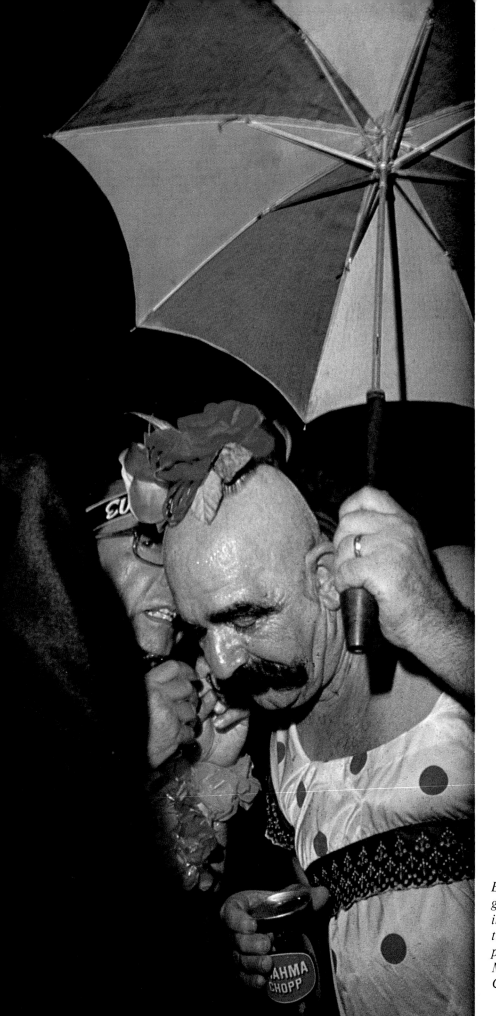

*Even in the past century, the great Carnival balls were held in theaters. Today this tradition is maintained by the presentation of a ball in the Municipal Theater on Carnival Sunday.*

Club dances are organized in all the districts during Carnival. Contrary to the custom in the early Carnivals, rather than hide behind an elaborate costume, the fashion today is to show as much as possible. *Previous double page: a group of harem girls at one of the club dances show their glittering beauty.*

*The Bahia wing of the samba clubs is one of the typical parts of the* escolas-de-samba *parade. Previous double page: marching down the avenue in the parade.*

*Hundreds of thousands of people take part in the parade, both as participants and spectators. But everyone sings and dances. Film makers come from all over to record the spectacle for the rest of the world to see.*

Like so many other monarchs these days, King Momo—the Carnival King—is merely a decorative figure. The only requirement is that he be fat. Previous double page: a cabrocha, in the midst of her samba club, dances in the street during one of the parades.

*Carnival has always been an important time in a Carioca's love life. During these three days of delirious freedom, many couples are formed, and many others break up. During the whirlwind of Carnival at times some are overcome by moments of tenderness or moments of sudden sadness.*

For all of the escolas-de-samba
the Carnival Sunday parade
down Presidente Vargas
Avenue is a time of long
awaited happiness. Many
march by weeping with
emotion. After the parade it is
as if a dream has come to an
end as well. Etched by fatigue,
a few faces reflect their
disappointment.

*The* escolas-de-samba *parade that starts on Sunday night always ends on the following morning, twelve or fifteen hours later, plus the preparation which had started several hours in advance. Parading several miles, singing and playing instruments before a crowd of thousands exhausts the Carnival dancer. He may sit down on any corner and fall asleep, perhaps to dream of the Carnival to come.*

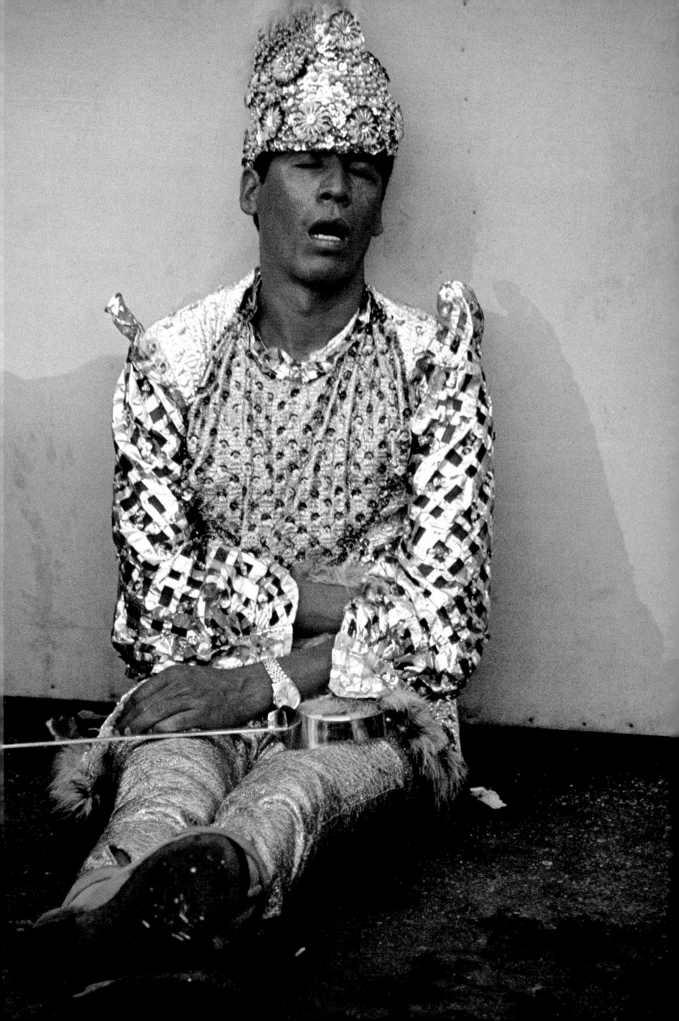

# The soul of Brazil

We now come to the end of our visit to Rio de Janeiro. In these pages we have walked down its streets and its beaches, climbed its hills and crossed the Arcos. From the top of Corcovado we discovered the majestic view of the city and the Bay of Guanabara, dotted with islands.

Perhaps the reader, with the help of our description and the beautiful photographs in this book can build his own image of Rio. But, alas, neither words nor photographs can replace the life or a city—especially a large city like Rio de Janeiro, where the stress of modern life has not suppressed the eternal quest of the individual soul nor dissipated its diversified cultural heritage.

That is why Rio, melting pot of all the elements that are Brazilwhite culture, African rites and music, Indian mementos—continues. All that is created or produced in the different parts of the country come to Rio to be molded and shaped into a product or an art form that no longer represents a region, but the nation. Rio forms the national character of Brazil. It is therefore impossible to imagine the Brazil of the future without the characteristics of this city and its people, who are more than anything else, a synthesis of everything that makes the country.

This historical role of Rio is even more evident when one realizes that it is the only great city in the world where popular beliefs and festivites still exist in every day life. They have not become anachronistic—they remain a dynamic factor in its life today.